Night of a Thousand Blossoms

ALSO BY Frank X. Gaspar:

A Field Guide to the Heavens

Mass for the Grace of a Happy Death

The Holyoke

FICTION

Leaving Pico

Night of a Thousand Blossoms

Frank X. Gaspar

Alice James Books   FARMINGTON, MAINE

10 9 8 7 6 5 4 3 2 1

Alice James Books are published by Alice James Poetry Cooperative, Inc., an affiliate of the University of Maine at Farmington.

ALICE JAMES BOOKS
238 Main Street
Farmington, ME 04938

www.alicejamesbooks.org

Library of Congress Cataloging-in-Publication Data
Gaspar, Frank
Night of a thousand blossoms / Frank X. Gaspar.
   p. cm.
ISBN 1–882295–44–7
I. Title.
PS3557.A8448N54 2004
811'.54–dc22   2003024340

Alice James Books gratefully acknowledges support from the University of Maine at Farmington and the National Endowment for the Arts.

Cover Art: "Moonflower and Copper Moth" by Anita Munman.
© 1994 www.20thcenturyfineart.com

ACKNOWLEDGMENTS

Grateful acknowledgment is made to the editors of the following magazines and anthologies where these poems (sometimes in earlier versions) originally appeared:

Bellingham Review: "Tacitus Considers a Poem in My Garden Late at Night"

Café Review: "Don't You Want to Walk Out Among the Lilies?," "Isn't It Enough?"

Gavea-Brown Journal: "I Am Not a Keeper of Sheep"

Georgia Review: "Hobbes," "The Persimmon Bough," "Can't You Hear the Wind Howl," "Paradise"

Green Mountains Review: "I Invite the Angel Gabriel, but Only the Wind Comes," "It Was So Dark Inside the Wolf"

Harvard Review: "It Is the Nature of the Wing"

Kenyon Review: "One Thousand Blossoms," "I Go Out for a Smoke and Become Mistaken for the Archangel"

Mid-American Review: "The Angel's Hand," "For the Womb Is a Great World"

Mosaic: "A Song for the Crows," "Flags Are Flying Everywhere"

Pearl: "Hurricane Douglas, Hurricane Elida"

Perihelion: "Bright Wings"

Pima Anthology: "Symposium"

Prairie Schooner: "Bodhidharma Preaches the *Wake-up Sermon*," "I Become a Disciple but Only in My Own Mind"

Quarterly West: "The Way That Can Be Spoken of Is Not the Way"

Revista Neo (Azores): "One Arm and Another Arm," "Tonight It's a Word," "The Ant," "My Hood of Stars"

Saber, Suplemento Acoriano de Artes e Letras: "The Lost Art," "You Can't Be a Star in the Sky Without Holy Fire," "Put Your Ear to the Ground"

Solo 5: "That Blue Rondo," "The Olive Trees"

Southeast Review: "The Blue Cigarette and Other Stories," "Castor, Pollux, Alhena, Propus"

Tampa Review: "There Were Footsteps in the Garden," "If I Looked for the One Art," "The One God Is Mysterious"

This book was written in dialogue with—and in homage to—a long list of authors, both dead and living, to whom I remain in obvious debt.

CONTENTS

1.   🍃   Jasmine

I Go Out for a Smoke and Become Mistaken for the Archangel   3
One Thousand Blossoms   5
Bright Wings   6
It Was So Dark Inside the Wolf   7
Hobbes   9
There Were Footsteps in the Garden   10
That Blue Rondo   11
The Lost Art   12
Can't You Hear the Wind Howl?   13
The Fruit Trees and the Junipers   14
Symposium   16
Isn't It Enough?   18
Tacitus Considers a Poem in My Garden Late at Night   19
I Am Not a Keeper of Sheep   20
Put Your Ear to the Ground   22

2.   🍃   Gabriel

Bodhidharma Preaches the *Wake-up Sermon*   25
Paradise   27
The One God Is Mysterious   28
The Work Was Too Easy   30

The Angel's Hand   31

There Is an Outcry in the Streets for Lack of Wine   32

My Hood of Stars   34

I Become a Disciple but Only in My Own Mind   35

The Ant   36

Castor, Pollux, Alhena, Propus   37

For the Womb Is a Great World   38

I Invite the Angel Gabriel, but Only the Wind Comes   40

The Way That Can Be Spoken of Is Not the Way   41

The Garden Will Come to You   43

3.   🌿   Green

The Blue Cigarette and Other Stories   47

The Persimmon Bough   48

If I Looked for the One Art   49

Just Now We Are Sitting in Sunlight   50

One Arm and Another Arm   51

The Olive Trees   52

You Can't Be a Star in the Sky Without Holy Fire   53

Flags Are Flying Everywhere   54

A Song for the Crows   55

It Is the Nature of the Wing   56

Don't You Want to Walk Out Among the Lilies?   57

Hurricane Douglas, Hurricane Elida   58

Tonight It's a Word   59

Many Trumpets and Maracas   60

The Sighing of the Ruddy Ground-Dove   61

Green   62

For Molly Malone Cook

No longer was the light the seat of the gods or their heavenly sign—over themselves they drew the veil of Night. Night became the mighty womb of revelations—the gods drew back into it—and fell asleep, only to go out in new and more splendid forms over the changed world.

—NOVALIS

"Sun, don't go!" I was awake
at last. "No, go I must, they're calling
me."
  "Who are they?"
      Rising, he said "Some
day you'll know. They're calling to you
too."

—FRANK O' HARA

1

Jasmine

Suppose you scrub your ethical skin until it shines,
but inside there is no music,
then what?
— KABIR

I Go Out for a Smoke and Become Mistaken for the Archangel

When I go outside on nights like this, nights without
cloud or breeze, city nights full of buzz and hoarse whisper
and the distant surf of automobiles breaking upon darkness,
do you believe I think the stars are waiting for me? How
lonely the streets are among the buttoned houses. How
I long sometimes for a doorway and a cigarette to smoke
in it, for some rain and a hat to pull forward over my eyes.
What is it in this darkness that draws the eye, anyway?
No blossoms shout color, no tree offers green in this
basin of shadow. Now all the requiems come forth, each one
with its measured voice, each ecstasy and lament, each
joy and despair joining hands. Who are these people who
have taped butcher paper across their front window and offer
me a shadow play I can't possibly forbid myself from watching?
The man is big bellied and sits in a chair. The woman is large
in the shoulders and sits in a chair. There is no other furniture
but a lamp and something—a pile of books? Newspapers? Who
can divine these shapes? By what right? Why are they rendering
unto the world so much of their unhappiness? Or am I
mistaken again? Maybe it's joy. In that other life, the hidden
life that counts, I walk across the gray lawn and tap at the window.
They mistake me for something I am not: a messenger, perhaps—
yes, a messenger. They come to the door and look and look
but they don't see me. And then they go back to their places
behind the window, behind the paper, in front of the yellow light
that deepens them and reduces them. And they have done
a good deal of work for one night. They have reduced me. They
have distilled me. It is a kind of resurrection and vindication.
Can you see it? It comes from that other life. You carry it with you,

you get used to it. You forget about it and it goes on talking and
singing and weeping all by itself. It's all right. It needs you.
You can walk me to the corner and share a coffee and tell me
your stories. It will still be there when you get back. It'll wait for you.

One Thousand Blossoms

Well, is it really wise to search for guidance in a small room
cluttered with books and papers, with a glass of whiskey
and a box of wheat crackers, with my eyes ticking like
the brass tide-clock on the plaster wall? When the house sleeps
huddled in the city's jasmine night? Night of a thousand blossoms
I can't name? Night of a soft marine layer, Pacific fog
hanging about a hundred yards up, a gauze, a parchment?
I am hidden thus from my duties, I can escape the moral law.
Isn't it written, didn't Lord Krishna himself say that we mustn't
relinquish the action we are born to, even if it is flawed?
Didn't he say a fire is obscured by smoke? You can't see far
into the city on a night like this, the blanket, the cool smell
of the sea, the dampness that sits like velvet on the rose bushes
and the African lilies and the fenders of the neighbor's truck.
You don't want less love—this ground has been covered before—
you want more love, even when you can't say what it means,
even though it binds you to the world, which you can only lose.
Then it is jasmine in the night, night of a thousand blossoms,
and my wife in one room breathing and my son in one room
breathing, and me in one room breathing. It's how loving this
place comes, slowly, then suddenly with great surprise, and then
vanishing again into mystery. Am I dreaming all of this? Is that
a train's long whistle riding the heavenly fog? Am I drunk again
on holy books and the late hours? Now a car rolls down the street,
filling it with light then emptying it again. It's like that. Just like that.

Bright Wings

Then I was walking in the garden looking for the intermediaries
between me and the clear light. Clouds of gauzy gnats flew up
and drifted in the buttery air. I had left the green hose running
much too long, and the earth was quenched and sagging under
the sweet peas. And something had been chewing holes in
the ear-soft leaves of the morning glories. Then I saw
for the first time that the neighbor was growing corn. Yellow
shocks were leaning just above the cinder-block fence, and they
looked so delicate and scruffy, like city corn, like alien corn,
and suddenly there was so much to be done, so much to put
in order—not the ordinary business of living and dying, but
the ordinary business that comes bundled with them. Sunlight
behaved perfectly in every corner. The shadows breathed in their
one direction and told stories. The cat crouched in the flower bed
aching to kill something. What is a man to do in such a moment?
When he knows he's being fooled by Heraclitean fire and all
those old and hopeful ideas about the moral jewel in beauty?
I mean in *this* day and age, when no one can even get those
equations to hold up anymore? Ants had formed a black
ribbon that led to a dead snail. And the Pipers and Cessnas
and Beechcraft were circling for the airport with so much color
and precision. And the dogs two houses down heard the mail-
carrier's foot and erupted. But these are not any answer I'm
looking for. *And I have been lazy.* Tangerines and lemons and
mandarin oranges have swollen and dropped from their impatient
branches. They lie among the fern and vine, bruised and mushy.
They are being swarmed. They are being devoured.

It Was So Dark Inside the Wolf

All day with nothing on my mind, the soft old couch,
the heating pad, a book of Tennessee Williams's letters,
tea, camembert, beer, soup, dozing, speaking in tongues
off in my drowsing mind, invoking this or that god, thinking
of raising my fortunes, thinking of all of this swimming forward
without me someday, this bag of small wishes, the greatest
sorrows indelible and indistinct in the afternoon's haze:
I cannot remember who said that our salvation must come
from a turn within our own nature and that there are no turns
and there is no nature. *Oh, it was so dark inside the wolf* said
the little girl with the basket after the hunters had killed
that beast who had eaten her, after they had cut him open to
let her out, although you don't hear *that* version so often anymore.
Surely this is significant. Who hasn't lodged in the belly
of something, who hasn't been devoured? Do you remember?
Maybe it is something for you like an old tune that haunts you,
that makes you so suddenly sad when you see a place where
the carpet is coming up or where the screen door is sagging
on a desperate hinge. Unbearable, this material music dissipating
the neighborhood around you into nothing. How does one rise
from this torpor and say, *I don't know what to do anymore?*
Outside the trees have sneaked above the line of the neighbor's
wall. How did I not notice? They make a tiny forest along
our city driveway. They are as dark and deep as it gets here.
I am still trying to rise up from the loveliness of dying objects
into the loveliness of whatever it is they point to. I'm trying
to get at just how things are, to adjust to that, but then I start
shaking. Isn't that how it is with you? It *was* so dark inside,
but that's not the whole story. They are leaving something out.
I can feel it in the sleepless night when I run my hands over
the openings in doorways. I can feel it when my own heart
delivers all my secrets to my enemies. I can feel it when

the poem doesn't turn but heads for the bottom with a hook
in its mouth or when the sky runs to the color of tin and
the sparrows disguise themselves as leaves in the hedge waiting
for their moment. Isn't that how it is with you?

Hobbes

For he can leap, but he doesn't bother with that too much—
mostly he sleeps or chatters in the windows at birds out on
the wires. I maintain that he is worthless, some misbegotten
kin to a possum, and in fact he came from a bad litter, a bad
neighborhood. There's something not right about him. How
then to name him *Hobbes,* as my son did, though I lobbied for
Meatloaf? We have an understanding. I don't make Hobbes
out to be more than he is: just some wild thing with an impossibly
tiny brain and no morals. For his part, he ignores me unless he
thinks I have food. I enjoy the purity of this contract, for it guides
me in my dealings with humans, which are few, at any rate, but
without much surprise or disappointment now that I've learned
not to expect others to be better than I am myself, now that I've
stopped raging at everyone else's smallness. We get what we
deserve, mostly. I won't say I learned this from a cat, I won't
try to make a tidy moral—nothing sweet or cloying. For he can
entertain himself by staring at the wall or licking his body parts,
which acts afford him great pleasure and from which I can derive no
honest instruction. And he brings grief and terror to the household
spiders, whom I have always liked, and so he places me in
an unsupportable position, a soft neutrality which ensures peace
in no corner, justice for none but the strong. My dream is to one day
be young and strong and garlanded with justice. Let the dead bury
the dead, let the sparrows and starlings compose their conga-lines
out on the boughs and conduits—it just might *be* a world without end,
feral and imperfect, though I admit I want to own it, I want to touch it,
I want to curl up in it and sleep in it forever, as though I am loved for
something beyond my control or choosing, as though even the dust
over my eye is what I am dreaming and I know exactly what it means.

There Were Footsteps in the Garden

I can't figure out the earth, everything saying yes and no
at the same time, everything shedding its hair and licking
its teeth and waiting to be eaten. And then there are the
great wings of the galaxies I'm looking at as they shudder
through the wilderness like spirits until they stoop through
my garden of lenses and mirrors. What is the loneliness
of all those shattered islands, what is so lofty, so hungry,
so intelligent, so needy about them? I'm reading in a holy
book about how the color red shifts and retreats in this
sidereal world, as though the stars are trying to hide
their forms from one another, as though they are afraid
of their nakedness—they all race away, and only the distance
grows, only the distraction, as if that were the point. Now
the yard is so quiet I can hear the snails being pulled
through the long grass by some reckless force beyond their
snail imagination. There are sayings now that would help me.
They would be nothing by daylight. The words try to avoid
embarrassment too. How can you blame them? But in
these pure hungers of the night it is another story. Precisely
another story, and then another and another. Oh, there were
footsteps in the Garden, all right. There was a firmament
hung with lights. But that was then. This is now. That's what
makes me ask for the *next* story. That's what makes me curl
in the blanket on the shivering grass and stare outward. That's
what makes tonight so safe for this one thing I'm trying to say.

That Blue Rondo

So where are all the planks in reason and those tapestries of paradise?
For I'm alone in the world and beyond even the most depraved
touch, here where there is no other life but in poems, where
even those citizens who write them are nothing but the breeze
that bellies through my window's raveled curtain or the shadow
of a moth buttering last autumn's jilted garden. And then here
is a sound I've never heard, a face I've never seen, this neighbor
over on the long street—he sits with a 12-string in his lap, slattern
chords, major and large under his wet sky, under his gruel-colored dusk.
Then I am grateful for the street and its mysterious trees, its
quiet righteousness. And I have stopped grieving the absence
of lilacs, the absence of forsythia, the absence of bayberry,
for all the wilderness here is strange forever, the sweet gum
and magnolia hand in hand with the eucalyptus and the sterile plum.
I have nearly stopped grieving for everything—or I have begun
to grieve for so much that I can't hear through the chorus. How
I envy, too, that guitar, the varnished bulk of its harmonies,
so utterly wrong for this street—not like the errant saxophone
six blocks down, its uncertain scales, not like the muffled piano
thumping *Rondo Alla Turca* from behind the old lady's peeling door.
What if the world really *were* filled with poems, like a snow of poems,
like all these leaves rising together in a green conspiracy at a given
signal in a given moment? Then I would choke on my own trials,
surely. Then I would find shelter here under the overhang of a porch
or under the awning of one of these bungalow windows. I would dry
my eyes. I would try my voice in all that hum and racket, though my words
would disappear. Though I would be dizzy. Though I would be singing.

The Lost Art

Surely it is too late to ponder this widening of the heart,
for the hour is uncertain, and sleep, that lost art, offers
no map. I cannot bear to think what brought me here,
under this fine shake roof, in this heaven of clapboards
and glazings. It's true, every word about love, every
syllable about longing—about how wanting anything removes
it to some insoluble distance. Where are my wise men now
when I need comfort? Where is the fine drug that slips me
from this world into its liquored shadow? Just now the moon
is razing the yard, lighting the crepe myrtle and the camphor
and the fey birches—now, when going out among those shapes
might be the one significant gesture. To think, someone
actually said our bones would rise from the earth—and meant it!
What is that rising now, then? In the night, the worm and
the beetle, and a nightbird I do not know, and the glow-eyed
things from the flood-ditches—the raccoons and possums all
citified and nervous, and nothing, nothing at all is bothering
to search for truth or meaning, because they are too busy, they
know that they must eat, and that when they slip, and they always
slip, there will be that hammer beak or the hairspring jaw,
or the palsy that binds like iron just before the dreadnaught wheels
and the numinous headlights that come on like time itself. It's all
so simple, except that it's not. So don't talk to me. Don't make
a noise. Step outside, onto the porch and be invisible, like I am.
Don't worry. Almost nothing is lost by this. This thing that
moves against your face is the wind—a breeze, really. About
that light in the sky you already know. Forget sleep, forget
the others—they aren't like you. Be still and watch and listen.
Then, without a word or a movement, tell me. Tell me how it is.

Can't You Hear the Wind Howl?

I'm shivering here with Coleman Hawkins and a cup of gin
and no idea what hour of the night it is—feeling ashamed
of how time passes when everyone knows I should be
the responsible party and put a stop to all this waste: What good
is a night if there's a dawn always lurking somewhere in the future?
How can I ever be completely certain of the stars if they fade
so easily before such cheap theatrics? When will I learn, as all
my betters have, to live in the moment? Out in the alley there's
a possum looking for a home. Out in the city lights there's an
alley looking for a street. You can hear the wind blowing
all along the window screens. It's singing to the voices in my head,
it's saying, *quiet!* It's saying, *Shooo!* Coleman Hawkins isn't
saying a word. He's occupied with some friends. He's living
in the moment among certain characters with names like Dizzy
and Django and Pee Wee and Cozy. He ain't going nowhere,
he is all past *and* future, if you know what I mean. I don't have
the nerve to say my heart is aching—not with *that* crowd all
around me, not with that bass line shaking the books in their
cracked spines and rocking the pens and pencils. Am I wrong?
Am I wrong to let Cicero rest awhile and to let Sappho, in her
tatters, sleep under the seven sisters, and to breathe in deeply
and to breathe out deeply? And to let the ice in my blue cup bark
in its quiet cataclysms and let the brown air blow down a hundred miles
from the deserts because I have no choice in these matters? Now
let me tap my foot in a certain way. In a certain way because there
was a machine once that could cull every kind of music from a room
and save it for a while, unharmed. Can't you hear the wind howl?
Here, all around my feeble senses? Here, in the iron lung of the night?
Here it comes again, all teeth in the palm leaves, looking for a home.

The Fruit Trees and the Junipers

Isn't something breaking down all over the city? I don't mean
the usual rant, all the rage and anger, the decent people muttering
in their coffee over in the Cambodian donut shop—not the slow
oxidation of absolutely everything, either. But one of the neighbors
is pouring out blood to the shades of the dead. I'm watching this.
She is lonely and wants information. My new young friend,
whose name I don't know yet, but who slouches and talks to me
in front of the YMCA, has opened a world. His tattoos are all blue.
His head is shaved. He and his friends cruise Huntington Beach
after the bars close, and try to bring people to Jesus. Today he tells me
he is throwing out all his old music. He is going to replace it with
new music. He has left some hard, mean life behind, this is obvious,
but we have not come that far yet. I don't know why I want this
sort of information, I don't know what my neighbor expects to learn
from a backyard of thirsty ghosts. Maybe she is just spraying for ants,
the way we all do, but she is so gray and alone with her husband dead
all these years, you can tell she is ready to board any bus that comes along
or take in one of these kids that come through the neighborhood at night
selling candy, strange kids, Black kids and brown kids, dropped off
from old gray vans. We are all concerned about them in one way
or another. Who is protecting them? Our neighbor would take them in,
I'm sure, but she is frightened of them, too. She has to be wary.
You can't blame her. I ask them, the kids, if they are all right.
Do they want a Coke, a glass of water? Where do they live? One told me
Chicago. Another told me New Mexico. What can this mean? They
always say, "God bless you," whether you buy something from them
or not. I am not so foolish as to refuse anyone's blessing, but I don't
know what they really mean, and when I bless them back, I don't
know what I really mean. Then when they are gone, the streets are
quiet again, quiet against that quickening hum of the city, that noise

that is always there, but never quite there. Then we close our doors
and go back to our lighted rooms. By then the neighbor has disappeared.
If I peek through a fingered slat in the blinds I can see her yard,
fruit trees and junipers all shadows in moonglow, and her small lawn empty.

Symposium

And now what is this nonsense with my left eye?
This land-mass that drifts over whole continents of
grammar and elaboration can not be a good sign: where
is that old vigor, that hard muscle? Where are the little
stories that render me untouchable by all the conventions
of the world of things? I'm reading about Eros when
the fog comes in. I can't tell if the wet heavy air out
under the sycamores is any more a hazard to clarity
than these renegade proteins gorging on my proper sight.
The suspense is killing me: How long will Socrates take
instruction from this Diotima, this woman, on the nature of
love? Won't he turn and devour her with his characteristic
sigh when the moment is right? But now she is telling him
how Eros demands that we beget in the beautiful, how Eros
of its own nature seeks what is immortal, in flesh and soul.
Why have I waited for September for all this? Why have
I left the summer behind with the same old scattered scraps
of paper, names, numbers, instructions to myself in every
humor and discipline, injunctions to be satisfied with nothing
less than First Principles? So that a cloud may drift over my
eye? Like a wing passing over a room's lamp? Here, by my
right hand, a glass of wine and a stack of bills. Here by my
same right hand another page of penciled notes, a stale cup.
In the late hush of the hours I can hear the frogs and crickets
in the flood canals, in the city's fruitful gardens. Do I dare turn
another page? Isn't it obvious that Law is not the measure of
good and evil? I am brought this way to my own hungers nightly.
I believe they are the same as yours, more or less, for who
will love us and save us, really? How will I lift myself from
one place to another by loving what I lack? How will you?
This is the way it goes in September, one page at a time, my
just portion of earthly matter floating like a dark island in the

middle distance of my vision, the distance diminishing or growing—
impossible to tell at this hour when the world of the hedge
and the lawn and the ivy has faded, when the streets are
muffled and softened, when the lights in the sky are amazed.

Isn't It Enough?

I know, I know, I am responsible for holding the stars
in their proper spheres, I am responsible for every symbol
in my own dreams, my accidents, my coincidences. How then
to explain this torpor, this lack of breath and sunlight when all
the streets are steaming from the recent rain, and the birches and
the sycamores and the chestnut trees are washed clean of their
leaves, and the leaves lie along the curbs in drifts, and the bare
limbs are smooth with muscles and tendons, white in the sky ?
Who would choose the spider? Who would get down on his
arthritic knees and choose the toad or the drowned earthworm?
I am off living beyond the normal mind again. I don't want
to give beauty back to God. What is owed is owed, what was
given was given: can't we leave it at that? I can't trust myself
to know what's expected of me. What lifts me up and makes me
buzz with splendor is not always good, nor goodness. It's too
much to bear, finally. I have to go out into the street and breathe
the newest air, the most advanced chemistry. The rain has fallen
and now it rises in a hundred fingers streaming into the afterlife.
Isn't it enough to walk under the arms of the great trees? Isn't it
enough to offer this confusion in its own chalice, for all it's worth?

Tacitus Considers a Poem in My Garden Late at Night

Such is the struggle, and such is the waiting
for the moment when something clear might strike—
have you seen the way a fruit tree shakes, late
at night when a possum is wallowing in its deep limbs?
At first it is terrifying. Tacitus says it reminds him
of what surrounded those Roman Soldiers he's telling
me about, the legions lost in the profound gloom
of the forests of Britain, and the leaves on the trees
moving, and the darkness of the wood and the darkness
of the enemy indistinguishable, every swish in the leaves
an omen of slaughter. But then this is California,
and Tacitus only sits on my chair in the little study,
face down, spine bent, pages dogged and yellowing,
and the sound in the trees is constant and unnerving,
but I know what it is, I've gone out before and shined
the lantern into the blood eyes, into the stubborn
wildness that doesn't yield or budge. All this time
I am sifting evidence, examining claims, though
this is not the fashion. So there is the struggle
and the waiting. Who can deny it? And who
can say what it is that moves like that—that cadence
among the boughs, the eerie shuffle—for I have fallen
back again into that old form of address, of saying
one thing is like another, and another and another
until all is lost. Oh, my possums. Oh, Varus,
the legions cut down and the thousands of corpses
draping the terrible trees! Tell them, Tacitus. It's
late here, and I'm waiting and struggling. What
would we do after all? What is it like out there, really,
above the garden wall? All the darkened trees are shaking.

I Am Not a Keeper of Sheep

Eu nunca guardei rebanhos,
Mas e comom se os guardasse.

How little I knew about the world when I let him in,
even though now I can't remember the day or time,
I can't remember what random thought guided my
hand in such an innocent act. I say this because it is
of no importance whatsoever on a hot August night,
a drink by my elbow, the cat speaking his mad language
against the window screens, and the blossoms of
so many papers and books in a desultory mess in the little
room. I have been reading without decorum or discipline—
the shelves are manic, nothing takes its civil place
according to alphabet or color or size. The center
cannot hold because it was never there in the first place.
One must never let Pessoa across the threshold. I can say
this with a sober mind for just a while longer. He sits
so unassumingly at the table and you give him a small
drink, and he begins to speak to you, and then you realize
your day is ruined, your plans will come to nothing, you
will end by trying every subterfuge you know to get him
to leave, but he will wait and wait. And he is so charming!
He will tell you stories, and you will recognize yourself in every
sentence—you will understand quite quickly that he his mocking
you, but then you will begin to doubt that, for he is so sincere,
so simple in his utterance, so passionate in his beliefs. How
can you not offer him another *cafezinho,* which I do, which
he sips noisily but with a certain finesse. Then I begin feeling
sorry for myself—that old sorrow—and I wish that someone
a long time ago cared for me enough to warn me, to tell me never
to let Pessoa into my kitchen, never to let him go on and on
about *his* sadness, that sadness that never leaves him no matter

how happy or content he feels, for then there is no hope for him
and none for me, and he at least has his genius to sit with, his
personalities, his Lisbon, his Tagus, and I, like you,
will have to settle for his company, wry, effacing, enigmatic,
too delicate for hearty jesting, too prickly and gloomy to be
of any real use around the house. Then the hours do not grow
late in the same manner. The rooms do not simmer and cool
in quite the way that I have become used to. The doors are
no longer silent on their hinges. The planks in the floor begin
their own conversations. So many things become impossible.
He drags a match across the abrasive strip of the matchbox.
The phosphorus makes its shushing sound. He lights another
cigarette. His fingers are so white, so slender, his wrist is like
a girl's wrist. *I am not a keeper of sheep,* he says. The night
will be long and soft with stars and the heat and the ticking
of one heart or another. He leans back in the chair with that
uncertain charisma, that narrow head. I can tell he is here to stay.

Put Your Ear to the Ground

The word on the street is loud. Today, stopped
at a red light, on my way home, I was judging
how eager I was, how willing, how deserving
to be at my high-piled desk writing poems—even
in my defunct idiom. I was thinking about my shame
at how that was the only task in this life I never grudged.
And the traffic was dense and lovely. Oh, the sun was like
oil on the flowers in the center divider, the breeze
moved like a salute through the gracious trees.
And then the ground heaved! And then the earth shook!
Drums and bass from a car window! This was Scipio's music
raising the hair on the soldiers of Carthage! This
was pain and suffering on a personal scale. This
was hunger, all around, no doubt and no argument.
This, I thought, will be a poem without an angel.
This concussion in the higher regions of decibels.
This call to you and me to attend to the other side.
This seduction to the long fall from paradise into
the garden of rage and the garden of muscle. Where
is the language for this? How can I tell you what
I mean when the bells are *still* breaking down their
own towers? I don't think for a minute there isn't
an ecstasy involved. I don't even think about holding myself
back with reason or faith. Have *you* figured out your
own single triumphant procession into the holy city yet?
What does that kid want, with his bandana and his tattoos, his
low car throbbing like a piece of fruit about to burst in the sun?
Listen. Put your ear to the ground, pass the messages
from hand to hand. There is a hunger all right. That's
what everyone's been trying to tell you. And it is
the *only* hunger, whether it's true or whether it's not.

2
Gabriel

You can't go neither forwards nor backwards into your daddy's time nor your children's if you have them. In yourself right now is all the place you've got. If there was any Fall, look there, if there was any Redemption, look there, and if you expect any Judgment, look there, because they all three will have to be in your time and your body and where in your time and your body can they be?

—FLANNERY O'CONNOR

Bodhidharma Preaches the *Wake-up Sermon*

There's no language that isn't the Dharma. Language is essentially free. It has nothing to do with attachment. And attachment has nothing to do with language.

—BODHIDHARMA

Somehow or another, something is missing in me. I should
be satisfied with the household gods. I should learn my place
and understand that they are enough for any one man or woman.
Of course we are at their mercy. They suffer us every small thing.
And we thank you, god of the kitchen drainboard and goddess of
the gas-log hearth. We thank you for your benevolence and kindness,
and god of the grocery sacks for your capacious heart, and goddess
of linoleum and green lawns, and winged goddess of the laughter
of neighborhood children, but always we are wandering from
your groves and bowers, your gardens, your abundant pantries.
For instance, what does anyone's life mean, now, in this third
millennium, so-called? I am talking about what you can and can't
live without, which is a way of talking about attachment. Is there
a language that isn't the Dharma? *To seek nothing is bliss,*
said the saint Bodhidharma, but isn't he the one who cut off his eyelids
in the search for a more perfect meditation? No, no, this is not
the way, in the heat of night, in the heat of fevers, the blue gas jets
wavering in the hot breeze on the kitchen range (goddess of
the four burners, goddess of the coffee pot, our acknowledgment,
our gratitude), not the way when we open the door to the small
empty street and look down its length, first one way and then the other.
It's what you can or can't live without. It's all streetlight and crickets
on this particular night. It's all language and breath in this particular
trial. It's all delicacy and power lines. It's all asphalt and glass. That's
why I am up night after night. That's why I walk so softly on the floors

and rugs. I am bowing and kneeling in every little corner, at every little helpful shrine, but I couldn't say if I am praying or if I am simply looking for some small button or short piece of string that I've lost. Most nights I really couldn't tell you what on earth I'm doing.

Paradise

I'm hoeing in the yard, in the beds where the fruit trees
and the heather are giving aid and shelter to a strange vine
that creeps upon everything, that will become my enemy
in time, I can tell, though now it is only probing the perimeter,
looking for weakness and opportunity. I cut with the hoe,
but gently, as though I might turn up something to save my life:
a jar of scrolls or a flint knife or a bronze spear-tip. But only
the worms show up, annoyed and pale, hustling to get back down
to their own secrets. I'm not paying too much attention this time
because I can still hear Beatrice and Dante talking—this is from last
night when, for lack of sleep, I dropped in on Paradise. Beatrice
asks Dante to let the fire of his consuming wish come forth, and
Dante begins talking about how a triangle can contain one obtuse
angle and no more. They are crazy in love, of course. Anyone
could tell. And it's Paradise, so she doesn't slap him or send
him to the store. No, love is impossible, it's an endless struggle,
and today nothing here loves anything, not the lemon or orange
or the purple blossom nor the fine pink worms. The world goes around
another way, and something about it doesn't care if you are drunk
on kisses or merely working outside in the summer afternoon. But
Beatrice knows something. I can almost make out what it is. Why
else would she be in Paradise? How else could she smile at Dante?
I know I'm wearing my Buddha nature like an old polyester shirt:
I should be completely mindful and absorbed by my task. Even
the Christians would agree, I should make my work a meditation.
But I can't seem to bend myself to these statutes today. I'm scratching
the black earth with an iron blade, but one fifth of me is in Paradise, one
fifth of me is on the verge of turning up all that news I've been waiting for.

The One God Is Mysterious

from an illustration of Babylonian sculpture

The king and his queen are feasting.
They recline, sumptuously, on long divans
and are attended by naked servants. They
can have anything they want, this much is
clear, and I believe they have been having
sex with one another and with the servants.
Why wouldn't they? Who among the servants
would not be honored to help? And it's Babylon
after all, and doesn't Babylon exist in your
memory? Isn't Babylon the clear rumbling
of your heart at ease with its every craving—
not the way it is now, fenced off with spiked wire
and old pipes, with signs telling the pedestrians
to beware: the litter, the old cans rusting. No,
this is my own memory of excess and extravagance,
of abandonment to the weight of everything
that pulls me down to ruin, those same ticks
and voices that lift me up and fill me with breath.
And don't you want to drink the breath of your
beloved? And his beloved? And her beloved?
You see how it goes. The One God is mysterious
and He has made me crazy. Maybe I am the king
or the queen. Or one of those sculpted figures
that bend so sweetly toward them, so graceful,
so finely formed and desirable in every way.
I remember being desired like that, and desiring
like that also. And I remember my heart in its deep
voice, commanding. Now that my common neighborhood
is tucked in for the night, the cars parked in the driveways,
the blinds drawn and everyone's drapes closed and the garage

doors locked, I can breathe easier. Now, in Babylon,
you see what is possible. The queen and her king are
dining, forever, in a gray frieze, but even so, they make
a fire in us, they free the ache from my shoulders,
they make every dark wish lie down with every bright wish,
they bring a great comfort to the harried in this land.

The Work Was Too Easy

Well, who am I to be reading Descartes at this hour, when
I can't even order my own mind? Or order my own heart?
And now that my sweet coffee has grown still and cold
in the blue cup, and now that all the lamps in the house have doused
and diminished to just my own, what can I hope to accomplish?
Perhaps it was the gloom in the sky this afternoon when I was hacking
branches from the idle poplar with my machete. It was my beloved
who wanted more light in the bedroom window, and the branches,
winter bare, were crowding and peeking. But, oh, what sadness.
The sky was like water, and the shadows so long. And the work
was too easy. But there in the narrow strip between our house
and the neighbor's wall, the earth was covered with leaves and
bark, all mulching down, in such natural order, such a melody of
browns and umbers, that I wanted to lie down too, and sleep awhile.
And how did I come by this small used copy, still marked one dollar
and fifty cents, a red cover with Descartes's face scribbled over in ball-
point pen? And why did my hand fall over it now, when there is
such melancholy in the air: the bare trees are despondent, the grass
is spiteful, the moon is soggy and blurred. I am quite sure of these
things. They are like music playing at the back of the house, distinct
but a strain to hear clearly. Yes, everything I ever knew was false.
But everything I ever knew was true also. Who hated you, Descartes,
who despised you enough to scratch away at your face, so somber
above your white collar, so melancholy, too—you can't fool anyone
about that, certainly not me. Now our little street is weary and cold
and damp in that manner of the California winter, and the houses
are strung with colored lights in praise of Christmas. And there is
a mist or fog that wants to settle over each green or red or yellow
tear. I am quite sure of this. If there were a coat at my feet I would
walk out again in the night's pure chill. And now if there were just
one song in my throat I wouldn't trade it for all the world's thinking.

The Angel's Hand

Consider the Prophet Ezekiel who ate a book. It was
filled with lamentations, mourning and woe, but
it made his belly feel wonderful, it was in his mouth
as honey for sweetness. And then John—John of
Revelations, eating that little book from the Angel's
hand. Oh, sweet as honey, he says, but then it made
his belly bitter. Why has it come down to me to make
sense of such things? All I'm trying to do is hold my
place in the world with a little grammar and a few pencils.
Before I go to bed each night, I make sure to look
for the stars, I make sure to read a little something, I
check the latches on the doors, I listen to the quiet, about
which so much has been written, this silence which is
layered with silences. And I have eaten many books. Some
were sweet in my mouth and some were bitter in my belly,
what of it? What of the Angel's hand? What of the chip
on my shoulder or the pain in my head? I'll tell you. I
will make something out of them. Maybe it will be part
song. Maybe it will be part honey and part gall. Maybe it will be
nothing but another silence in the night of a thousand silences.
Maybe you will take it and eat it, and then before you go to bed
you will check the latches and you will listen out your windows.
Maybe then you will be the one to make sense of such a thing.

There Is an Outcry in the Streets
for Lack of Wine

You can accuse me of putting bitter for sweet,
but I'll defend myself and say that I put sweet
for bitter also. I put sweet for bitter whenever
I can, and I can say it has covered my sorrows
when there was not a single other way out, no
other way to lift myself and stand again, and I have
to stand again, even though I get weary and I stumble,
even though the arrows of the world are sharp.
I understand the danger of speaking directly, but
I believe I am still within all the conventions: I've
read your verses, Isaiah, and I find a certain quality
of mind in them, a certain passion—I'm being obvious
but I'm trying to get to know you, your face
for instance, or your work habits, or your mental health.
And your lines! How they cheer in all the wrong ways!
There is an outcry in the streets for lack of wine!
Or, *the wine mourns, the vine languishes!* Where
is the feint? Where is the subterfuge? Nowhere.
I don't know whether to believe you mourned and
languished, but then, why not? Who hasn't? And
yet, there you are, teaching me a certain hardness,
a certain way of standing so that I can't be rocked
by a punch, so that I can't be thrown. It doesn't matter
that I'm twenty-seven hundred years too late, that I have
a different slant on things. So let me say sweet for bitter:
I can't speak like you, beyond the sacred halls of all those
thousand ruined choirs, but I say sweet in the morning
over coffee and in the evening and in the deep night when
you and I stare at one another across all the difficulties.
Of course I'm dismayed. Of course I'm confounded.

I know the grass withers and the flower fades. But
I can measure the sweetness. Like that sound in your
lines, so brutal, so tender, so ready to be misunderstood: I
can hold it tonight like wild honey on the back of my tongue.

My Hood of Stars

God was still walking around in the wilderness
fascinated and puzzled. He kept trying to show
me how to take the words from dreams and old
magazine covers, to make something out of them.
He was preoccupied for hours and hours, but
he never spoke his mind plainly. He did not
like people to feel too comfortable around him.
He was far more troubled than anyone now wants
to remember. This is when the world was
mostly without form, but it wasn't void: it is
just that everything made only one kind of sense.
You didn't have good words like *automobile* or *deduction,*
though you had *rebuke* and *anoint.* Then God
bent down and picked up a handful of desert.
Not really. It's just how we talk about such things.
He picked up a handful of desert and there came
a great tempest. Then there were worlds standing in line,
waiting on street corners and in train stations. Then
God went a great way into that wilderness, whistling
and singing in bright garments. I watched him go.
Everybody did. Then his stars fell around us like swallows,
stricken and stunned: That's when the people began scooping
them into their pockets and purses, trying on names, in-
venting excuses. That's when I tried on my own garment,
drunk on fear and craving. That's how *I* began whistling and singing.

I Become a Disciple but Only in My Own Mind

Now everything I love is out of fashion. The Buddha
was telling us about the Eightfold Path, and he was
explaining Right-Mindedness. This was in English.
This might have been in a garden or a gentle wood
watered with bright springs. The Buddha explained
that I must keep a pure and thoughtful mind. But
I was polluted with desire for the world and its delights.
I still am. I drive an old Jeep and wear sunglasses. I throw
myself into the ocean every chance I get, and I wait
as long as I can to ever shower the salt from my body.
I make every excuse. Sometimes I am seized with great
lamentation for the smallest reasons: a candy wrapper
in the wastebasket, a pencil with a dulled point, the noise
our refrigerator has begun making every so often in the night.
How simple, says the Buddha: *the senses are the cause of suffering.*
He wants me to go off and sit under a tree with him. How
can I resist him? He is so serene and powerful. And he
needs me, he needs to enlighten me, you can feel it all around
him, and the tree is an incense tree, and finches and sparrows
are chirping. It is summer. There is salt on my body, everywhere.
The Buddha and I sit quietly. The sun is bathed in a glory
of orange clouds. I want to ask him the difference between
my ecstasy and my despair, but I keep to my silence. His face
is a mask. He would never answer me. And I can tell he might not know.

The Ant

In the Glorious Book, the Glorious Verses,
which the Angel Gabriel labored over, bringing
Mohammed along slowly, sound by sound,
letter by letter, such are the Scriptures: *And the ant*
was told to take his legions out of Solomon's
way lest the ants be crushed unknowingly. Some
of us sat uneasily at our small desks. This was
during the first lessons. It was hard to absorb things.
We stifled our questions, which were many.
We were befuddled by the all the glory.
We were worried about the Prophet—He wanted
to get everything right, He tried so hard. The rest
of us were ashamed of ourselves, yet happy for Him.
And so now when an ant comes into the house
I never rush to the usual poisons. I always speak
a warning first. I importune the ant to take away
his legions. Coincidence is a word that no longer serves
me well—I have been won over to that. But the ants
keep their own counsel. Then I am so alone in the universe,
so hot and sticky in summer, so resolute and wavering by turns.
In the breezeways, in the pantry, in the windows behind
the whitewashed sills, the ant and his legions, and the Angel
and the Prophet—they carry on far into the night, under
the moon and the alien stars. When I hear the great arguments,
I still comprehend nothing. When I can no longer tell
who is speaking or who is singing, I lie down on the cool tiles,
where the voices and the endless lessons never let me sleep.

Castor, Pollux, Alhena, Propus

Now there is complete madness under the spring stars of Gemini,
for something is breaking the darkness into a thousand greedy songs.
It is a thousand crickets chirping and a thousand frogs peeping,
making up another swarm of stars. Never mind that the gloomy
mosquitoes are whining up from the flood canals, full of cravings—
they are praising the darkness, too, they are taking their hidden
lives and splitting the world into all these tireless cantillations. What
care you must take, walking out to the camphor tree to break a branch
and breathe its molecule into your own flesh! How cautious you
must be to not be swallowed whole by such a time as this, how wary
to sidestep the desire to try to steal some of this world, to try to take
it down like shorthand or rhetoric, to a place in your mind where your
practical addictions will try to parse the voices and render comment.
Anyway, those are the warnings I give myself, late in the shadowy
yard, standing in my uncertain skin, leaning on my complacent bones.
Let the night go on forever, or for a few more hours. Some creatures
understand that the day, with its glare and logic, was made for rest.
Some creatures understand nothing, of course. They don't need to.
The stars come out and bid a choir to sing. It is the first choir and
every other song is just an answer offered up to its secrets. You can
watch and listen, but don't think too much. First the sky bleeds itself
to its earliest darkness, and then the planets and the brightest stars assure
you that they have always been there. When it is safe, the others come
and show themselves, and then that singing fills every shadow. Don't
worry about it. Don't join in. Don't go counting hours and minutes,
don't wait for the Angel, don't go naming God. Just breathe. It's enough.

For the Womb Is a Great World

For when the body was formed, a Soul was formed, and
when the Soul took shape in the body, the Body formed
the Vital Spirit. And when both had taken shape, the
Womb was formed. For the Womb is a great world, there
is no world more powerful than It.
                    —From the GNOSTIC GOSPELS

Do not write this poem, says a voice just behind my left ear,
but how shall I trust it? How will I know what's real and what's
false in any honeyed night or, for that matter, in any summer day
when the sun is shining and the wind is blowing off the ocean
and shaking the garden leaves? For the womb is a great world,
yet where will I find such a world except without me and beyond me?
Oh, *the male organ is vigorous* saith the scripture, on page one hundred
and thirty nine—*it is the channel of mysteries*—they give us that—*it is*
a wellspring, but it is not a great world, ask any lover after the glow
has departed and he or she will tell you. I should not write this poem.
How to fathom the minds of the Gnostics? And why? How to grasp
that the anus is the *first mouth*? How to understand the instruction
concerning erections, concerning the right way to release the seed, and
what do they mean by being *orderly in the act*? This is a far cry
from all those epistles written by my old friend Saul of Tarsus. Oh,
so much was lost when the Gnostics were thrown out, but what exactly
I cannot tell. Who in the age of the neutron and the neutrino can know
precisely what takes place when *the Spirit sings a hymn to the Soul*? But
what a well-dressed way to talk about these yearnings I have, this tropism
that brings me so easily to my knees, what a way to make good on my
most sweeping desires, to claim a place for myself on the sweet belly
of the earth where I am told I belong, though I am often told otherwise,
and where I move lightly, with heed, and such dream and bewilderment.
Do not write this poem, says the voice behind my ear, but I

am headstrong and swept along by the idea that *the Power of Light divulged itself and Radiance became manifest, and the Womb is a great world, and the breasts are two worlds, and the two thighs are two worlds, and the hair of the whole body,* and it is far too late.

I Invite the Angel Gabriel, but Only the Wind Comes

The wind again, this time wheeling down from the northwest
and dumping rain, the wind-chimes in the yard banging like hammers
and the gates slamming on their hinges. And then it has passed
and it's time to go outside and walk the winter grass, the color now
of old celery and cardboard. The yard is littered with tangerines,
hard and green. Now it's time to advance and gather them up. I am
not the chosen one to whom the Angel speaks. I don't mind. I don't
believe I could bear up under that kind of pressure. I don't mind
speaking to the Magnificence, night after night, without an answer.
Something was loose in the yard, that's clear—something that asks
for a new way of speaking, which I haven't figured out yet. Here
is a shingle gloved in moss and here is a branch in white fracture
recalling a human bone, and here is the sun breaking the cumulous
tower and here is the heart I abandon more or less regularly, lying
in a nest of wet leaves. I don't mind. I pick them all up. I carry them.
I say a few words, but only in the eternal space in my head. It's fine.
The sun keeps shouldering through, the crows are finding their wires,
the sparrows are eternal. The air is charged with incongruous smells,
clean linen, for instance, and sharp oxygen, and wet earth. I am
a presence among the scoured ruins. It's time to stoop and collect.
It's time to be quiet again, and poke and prod. It's time to find
baskets for all this smitten fruit, round and perfect and shining.

The Way That Can Be Spoken of
Is Not the Way

Once again the tropical air comes cruising in
from the west-southwest of Baja. I'm looking
for accidents as though they might speak to me
in some revelatory tone. The sky is so unusual
with its high, chalked scud. The heat. The rare
humidity. All afternoon I have been talking about
paradox. I have been reading the *Tao Te Ching*
with young men and women who are in love with it
for a while—just now when they are away from their
jobs and families and friends. But I can tell they
are looking for accidents, too—they want to *know,*
even the two boys who are so angry at the world
that they refuse to honor justice as a concept. They
insist that morality is an agreement. Ah, well, we
haven't gotten around to reason yet. We haven't
talked about the Forbidding Principle, but we
are talking about appetite: everyone says, *oh,
sex,* and then we laugh, and then I say *ambition,*
and they laugh. And then someone says—it's
inevitable—someone says, *Isn't it just whatever you
want it to be? Isn't it just whatever you think it is?*
But that will come later. Now the icy wind
is whipping through the air conditioning duct, and
the flesh on the young arms puckers and is lovely.
Off in the windows a couple stands by a blue bicycle,
but I can't see their faces. The heat makes certain
things shimmer. The brightness outside the room
is painful. That too will come later. There is a sudden
weariness that dresses me right in front of their eyes,
but I don't let on, I don't throw myself back in the chair,

I don't press deep into my own eyes with the heels of my
hands and breathe with despair and happiness both
in the same moment. *What,* I ask, *is The Way?*
Is it a force? An entity? A method? And who,
I wonder, has already begun to hide from his own
longing, or her own wishes, which are probably not
dark, not dark or untoward? What is there left
to simplify? Isn't this some kind of wisdom, this
inability that they have to keep still? How they chew
their pencils, how they lean, how they shuffle. Who will be
my teacher in this late afternoon? How foolish I feel
for wishing that I still knew the things they know. They
breathe the cold air. They wait for the endless news.
And then they are gone, out into the endless day. That heat.
That wisdom. That unbearable light. It's just what they think it is.

The Garden Will Come to You

Now we have installed our little Buddha in the yard, under
the camphor tree and the Chinese cherry, where he sits at peace
looking rather like one of the gray river stones in his vicinity,
except for his posture and his crown chakra, which reaches
toward heaven like a topknot above his smooth forehead. Here
is a mind where the vermin and roaches lie down with the angels
and priests. Here is a trick I'd like to learn. Is it true that now
every tuft of lawn and viol of hollyhock lean toward the Master
in deference? Or is that another trick? When the mud-colored
doves descend from the wires and disappear in their camouflage
into the furrows of the hoed earth, the cats are not fooled, nor
does anything weep for their certain pounce and the torn wings
and the soft down drifting over the early grass in a distracting snow.
No, the way is to be at one with things. The way is to sit in the padded
chair with a little gin or tea and to contemplate my lucky bones,
so full of the earth's heavy stuff, and my own mind, with its faint
lightning, and its own roaches and angels, which are glorious, both,
because they are mine. They owe me so much. I don't move.
I don't collect my debts. If you asked me for a stone, I just might
give you a loaf by mistake. Don't despair. Don't lose yourself
in all these daily vexations. You'll see, if you are still, if you are disciplined,
that the garden will come to you. It will grow around you, vine by branch.
And the leaf at your throat which rises to smother you will also cloak you
and then you may relax, you may disappear in a world of green
where you and all your chores mean nothing. See the little Buddha?
See the buds and runners of spring? Sit quietly. This is the only way.

3
Green

Light wrestling there incessantly with light.
Star kissing star through wave on wave unto
Your body rocking!

— HART CRANE

The Blue Cigarette and Other Stories

Oh, that was a more innocent time, a more innocent world,
I can't dispute it, when it was possible to turn my collar up
against the weather and put a cigarette between my lips,
my hands cupped around the match—I was ready, then,
for some adventure, for some of those drug-store prophecies,
for some foray into the street or down to the pool hall,
or later, with those horrifically sad bar-girls in their
bright silk skirts, always hustling drinks, always trying
to get me upstairs. No gaiety about this, just the cigarette
against my tongue, the blue smoke curling up past one eye
or the other, and sometimes the wonderful lace of opium,
or even when I used to just pinch the desolate roach of a joint
into the end of a Camel and walk through the park, smoking,
high, the civil twinge in my lungs. What happened? All those
times have collided now, without any gist or sequence,
and dreams, too, wear their deceptive coats and shoes and
sit like perfect guests on the stuffed chairs and sofas—no one
can sift the first real thing from any other real thing, surely
I can not with my drifty nostalgia, which I excuse in myself
but would probably not forgive in you or any of your friends.
But am I not justified? You stoop after beauty, only beauty,
pure beauty—and where does that leave you? Isn't it written
that on a specified day every prophet will be ashamed of his vision?
That's how it was from the beginning. Aren't you tired of a language
that takes no risks, spoken by persons who have taken no risks?
Weren't you the one trying to make out signs in the feeble streetlight,
in the gauzy rain? Yes, the tough girls, the lovely boys, the rage,
all that business they always called love. And me with my
cigarette, the tip sweet in my bitter mouth, and that match just struck
in its sulfur and its brashness, that match in my fingers, flaring.

The Persimmon Bough

And now it's the night of the weeping persimmon, night of the lights
in the sky, both the stars and the airplanes, night of the beautiful
siren and the dog so far away he sounds like the dog in the moon.
And here is the complacent toad and the ungloved bat—they are
coming to take the high road. And here is the porch lamp gleaming just
bright enough to cast shadows on the grass—it is showing the way.
And here is the little black-bound notebook, eating its words. They are
delicious and please the tongue and try to seduce the world, and then the
world slips away singing its song, and I follow after it even as it becomes
the trees and the houses and the rustling leaves again. I admit it— I love
my earth in this fashion. Everything I need is at hand. If a poem
says kiss, then I kiss. If a poem says weep, then I weep. If I must put
my heart away, I put it away in the night where I am sure to find it again.
Just now the yard becomes hushed. The siren and the dog have crept
into the black-bound notebook and are silent. Their silence exhales
into the adjoining yards. A late window shines through the curtain
of ficus leaves, like a light in the forest, but this is only a neighborhood
two blocks off the avenue, and the distance is deceiving. And I took
a chance. The persimmon tree, for instance. It was never weeping.
It was just leaning its lovely limb over the cinder block wall, it was
just letting its fruit down low. If God was saying something, we all
missed it. We were all looking at one another, we were all charmed
with one another, swept up in the peace of one another's easy swaying.
So I take another chance. Velvet, diamond, ruby, emerald night—what
is true among all these changes? The siren again, and the dog again,
an airplane winking—almost like a star, and the brilliant languor of the
persimmon bough, a cascade, like a woman's long veil, like tears falling.

If I Looked for the One Art

Then I am adrift in the world and am curious as to its blessings,
which are so often dark and random, so often like the arrows
and the spears of the old poems, so often like the wounds
and cries of the old songs. If I looked for the one art,
where would I find it? How would I know it? If you were
my brother in this struggle, how would you stand by me? If
you were my sister in these vanities, how would you direct me?
Now it is necessary to turn from the December night in its rich
and promising darkness, its accurate stars dunning the earth,
its lace of chimney-smoke among the stripped gum trees. I know
I can't live in ecstasy—I wasn't built that way. I know my
sorrow is such simple chemistry. I know my heart will always be
desperate because that's what it's for. Where is it, this one thing that
is so true—not by degrees but by absolutely vanquishing every sense?
Is it in the yard or the fallow garden or under the pitched roof?
Maybe it's in the wind, that wishes it could bluster, you can tell,
but only wishes and wishes. Maybe that's it. Here it comes
again, a sound in the bellied wires, in the raked antennas, in
the bare hedges, where anyone can see there should be only nothing.

Just Now We Are Sitting in Sunlight

All the late morning and one sound has been calling
to another sound. My beloved tells me they are doves,
the gray doves, the plain doves we sometimes see on
the backyard wires—or sometimes see lying ripped open
like pillows by the street's marauding cats. My beloved
is more like a cat than a dove, but she is dove-like, she
is dove-like in the morning when she settles into her nest
of quilts and books, so many books, which sometimes
become heavy and lay themselves down on her breasts.
Oh, she is like a roe and a tower too, I am sure. But just now
we are sitting in sunlight and the wild voices are crying
to one another. Spring was late this year, if we can be said
to ever have a spring. The ocean was colder than usual
which may have vast implications. Now in fall the ocean
has become as smooth as a lake and we don't go to it anymore.
We are always at the mercy of so many currents. We are no longer
young. I don't believe that we regret much more than anyone else does.
Sometimes we drive the avenues and wander through bookstores
apart from one another, out of each other's sight, and when
we meet we are like strangers, shy and stand-offish. But just now
we are sitting behind the windows, and there is the one sound
calling to the sound that answers, and my beloved, among her books
and quilts, whose hair shines in the yeasty light, tells me they are doves.

One Arm and Another Arm

Deve haver um lugar onde um braço
e outro braço sejam mais que dois braços
—EUGENIO DE ANDRADE

One arm is pulling another arm's weight. It is not a burden,
it is not something onerous, for one arm loves the other arm,
loves its skin and all its intricate mechanisms, its long truths
and its falseness, which it recognizes, in its wisdom, as another truth.
Then we are moved to a place where one arm and another arm
can be more than two arms, for it is autumn and the leaves,
in this part of Earth, are not bursting with brilliance, but simply
letting go. They drift into small piles along the sidewalks, along
the narrow driveways and bungalows. They no longer wish
to be a burden. They want to sleep in the gutters because
they are overcome with the beauty of the lowering sun, the
light that has taken on a whole new slant—new in their short
lives. You could say they are lying in one another's arms. This
is the idea that comes to me, and then the only question is where
can this be, this place? It's not in the world outside the windows,
and it's not in the world inside the windows. Maybe it's in
the sleep that hangs around my head and lifts all its fevers. Maybe
it's that very light, so low in the air, so true in its arcs and angles.
Would it make you ever want to lie down among the dry leaves,
but in your mind only? Would you find there the arms of all
the beloved, loving still another and another? If this isn't the false
idea or the true idea, then would you ask me to name this place?

The Olive Trees

In the campus courtyard, in the center of the oldest building
of all the old Spanish buildings, among the white
stuccoed walls, among the ochre tiled roofs, the olive trees
are preparing to leave this world. They are dropping
the dark boles of their olives. They are lightening their burden
as if they might straighten their scarred backs. And the olives
are everywhere under the feet of the young girls and
the young boys and under the shoes of the old men
who are stooped with the weight of their books: olives
like black stars or black fish, staining the brick, drawing
the gnats and the resolute sparrows. The olives are bitter.
You cannot eat them. Here in the sun, on the weathered
bench, I cannot think how Claudius Caesar could have survived
alone on the secret olives he plucked from his trees, when he knew
his wife had poisoned his meals for weeks on end. Yet he outlasted
her resolve. That is the story. But these olives are bitter and
you cannot eat them. And where can they think they are
going, these bent, decrepit trees? See how they cast away
their eyes and ears. And the young, crushing them under
their soft, light feet, and the old, crushing them under
their heavy heels. These trees! See how they think they
have had enough of the earth? See how their shadows
are merely lace, how they leave the morning sun unperturbed?
See how they ready themselves over and over for the new life?

You Can't Be a Star in the Sky Without Holy Fire

Why should I keep telling you what I love, and whom?
I am so dull and awkward, what difference would it make?
Yet I can't shut up. I'm like that mockingbird up on the
bee-riddled pole at the corner of our easement. He is de-
mented, singing *I must have sex,* singing *stay away from me.*
Every once in a while he does a little hip-hop, he flaps his
wings, he does a break-down. When does he breathe? When
does he sleep? And beneath him are the morning-glories,
who could teach me a thing or two about the absolute rage to live,
and also the trumpet-vine, which is serene and alluring, but which
is all muscle and will underneath. And the wisteria! You
would stand naked in the snow-white shower of its blossoms, but it
would send a root down through you and plant a stake in your heart.
No, I can't shut up, it's not in my nature, just as beauty is not,
just as all those virtues I read about have gone missing. And I
don't want everyone to gather around either. In another world
I am ready to lie down in solidarity with all the doomed blossoms
along all the white fences. In another world I would stop grinding
my own bones. In another world I would convert all my failures
and consume them in a holy fire. But then there is that mindless
bird—he can't shut up—and it's one world only, and he knows it.

Flags Are Flying Everywhere

How public this sudden happiness, how unseemly,
the sun getting low in the west beyond the Boeing office towers,
and the college lawn striping itself with the shadows of the long trees—
the science building, too, the tall birches rising against its
white and brick bulkheads for no reason. Flags are flying every-
where, every house, every porch. The sun is changing the color
of everything—the air is ablaze with a shine like autumn fruit, like
the leaves of the maple and the sweet gum that drown in their own
decadent senses, that say, "take me," and are taken. Two boys
come clowning up a broad empty walk, one upon the other's back.
A slender girl with books in her arms is skipping beside them,
yelling in a language I don't know about. They are on fire, too.
They are warm in the light. I think this is their way of saying
thank you, or perhaps, *I am falling in love with this world.* But
one can't be sure. Maybe they are caught up in a kind of striving and
I am caught up in a kind of terror. Certainly we have all moved into
a time where nothing can be completely trusted: The automobiles
are roaring in the street, the chrome is gleaming, but you can't count
on it. None of the little poets talk about joy anymore. No one is blessing
the glass or the fenders nor the slight modest squirrels nor the feral cats
that watch them without mercy from under the skirts of the privet hedge.
And no one is visiting *me* with any special kindness or attention, but nothing
stalks me to ravage me either, except my own ghost, which resembles
a shadow this afternoon, stretched, a trifle comic, something that only
makes me smile far away inside my head. The buses moan in their
wreaths of blue smoke because they have to. The pennants snap
in the upper wind because they are powerless. Every mote of dust lands
precisely where it is supposed to because of the ancient instruction. When I
move over the grass I am either the light or the place the light will never reach.

A Song for the Crows

The crows are ferocious, cleaning my roof this morning.
This is no time for desolation and mistrust, but for study
and sobriety. I can let go of the morning ache for awhile.
I can stand for a moment at peace with crow muscle
and crow wit. The wooden shingles are rife with
nourishment, but I cannot divine its nature from here,
in the driveway, where I stand, still and cautious, not willing
to give the skittish crows a reason. For they are banging
the roof with their dagger beaks. From inside it sounds
like a carpenter's hammer, or else it sounds like someone
rapping to come in and sit by the stove for coffee. But now
I am under the sycamore, I am an eye for the crows, they
do not meditate, they do not behave gently. I understand
how I want to write close to song, but I do not understand
how the crows can have no song but the one I will give them:
They are so replete with their imperatives and their questions,
their logic and geometry. They make a form on the roof.
I believe it would be a grave mistake to count them.
It would be equally wrong to admire them, though they
shine like stones taken from deep out of the earth,
and there is something iron or granite about them in their love
for God, which I can infer by the mass of their bodies and
by the way they reach into silence and find utter certainty,
by the way they will not wish and will not regret. Then
it doesn't matter that in a sudden gust of breeze, the dry leaves
rustle, and the crows lift and scatter and labor their way
over the neighborhood fences. It doesn't matter that I am left
to myself now, and to my intentions and to my misdemeanors.
This is how I am at home with the concrete and the visible.
This is how I understand that this is not a song for the crows.

It Is the Nature of the Wing

The problem is being a fragment trying to live out a whole life.
From this, everything follows. Or the problem is being
fractured and preoccupied with one's own mending, which
lasts as long as you do and comes with its legion of distractions.
Just now, when a lovely-throated motor comes gliding up
the street to one driveway or another, I can tell you
there is a certain kind of safety in a fact like that. It is so
solid you can lean on it in your bad hours. It can lift you, too,
from your despair, which is of no consequence, which can
be measured against the dropping flowers of the wisteria,
which fall because of their nature and essence, and stain
the redwood planks of the small deck in the back of the house.
That doesn't mean those used-up blossoms feel at home
under everyone's feet or at the mercy of my stiffened broom.
Didn't Plato say it is the nature of the wing to lift what is heavy?
He was speaking of love again, I can remember that much, and
then love was a ladder, too, but lifting again, always upward.
Then it is possible to love Plato for his faith, which is so strong
he becomes difficult and obdurate in the late nights. He is
hardly distracted by a passing car. He is fixed on something
beautiful, and why not? When I step out onto the porch, there
is nothing shining in the sky. Oh, and the wisteria blooms have
fallen some more and are like a sad carpet. And some small
insects are dancing in the garage's yellow lamp. They don't hear
the little bats squeaking. It's all right. You could even say they
look happy, they look joyful. Surely they are beautiful in their
ignorance and danger. See how they hold your head and command
your eye? Looking upward? Looking toward that homely light?

Don't You Want to Walk Out Among the Lilies?

It must be one measure of the global warming, how all
the little bookstores have gone away, and now there is only one
bright, gaping cavern of books, with its parking lot and the gray-
bearded man in the taped-together eyeglasses and army fatigues
with *Jesus Wept* stenciled in black on the name patch over his pocket.
How he has gathered so much authority unto himself with his
Windex and newspapers and squeegees, so that when I give him
a dollar, and he says, *God bless you,* I believe in him completely
though I can tell something is not right about him, life
has not been good to him, he has missed many opportunities.
And the bookstore! With its bins and shelves and coffee and culture.
You can buy all the holy books, you can browse the Scriptures
on the second floor and take your tea there. Is this not useful?
Can't you breathe easier among the pages and pages smelling
of ink and glue and fingerprints? So when I'm on my knees
among the stacks humming to the Buddha, or mumbling
to the Prophet, or swaying to the Psalms, don't judge me. When
I puzzle over the Sutras, leave me to my defects. When the hour
is right, we can lay ourselves down on the carpets and rugs.
When the world considers us from a distance, we will be without
consequence, we will be nothing. Then there will be no weight
that we can't bear up. There will be no message that we can't unbind.
Don't you want to walk out among the lilies of your city and
save every perishing thing? It is all so terrible and so simple.
Let's put down the cross. Let's lay down our burdens. It is sweet,
this land. Walk with me out among the cars and the sodium lights.
I don't know what lies beyond that visible hedge. It doesn't matter.
It will be milk. It will be honey. We can go there together.

Hurricane Douglas, Hurricane Elida

Here they come again, those Pacific hurricanes,
and here I go in my old white Jeep, sandy and musty
with boards and wetsuits and damp towels, down
the boulevard, down the bougainvillea and the jacaranda,
the red lights and green lights, the Shell station and
the Union 66 station, the 7-11, Anna's Escrows,
Pacific Coast Medical Group, Tiny Naylor's Restaurant,
the Los Altos YMCA, houses and houses behind their
honeysuckled walls, and rows of palm trees curving up
to the muggy sky. A left turn on the highway and watch
the rivers in their concrete bunkers, glassy now because
the wind has not shifted onshore yet. Good. And then turn
toward the pier and wedge into a parking space and then
down the sand, and there they are again, rolling in like
boxcars, swell after swell, angling off the bar under the pier,
half-again over my head, and then for the first time ever
the thought that I am too old, too weak, too short of breath.
This is fear. How comely, how appealing it is! How
it slows me pulling on the wetsuit and fins, waxing the board,
how it makes my pragmatic heart so ready, knocking against my
ribs in a way that I can hear it all the way up in my head. But
Bang Bang go the breakers, and in *I* go and dig in with my arms,
and get stuck inside a big set, pulling and pulling and getting
nowhere, duck-diving under the whitewater, heaving a breath
into myself when I come up, digging again to take back the distance
I've already lost, digging and breathing like there's no turning
back because, after all, there isn't now, and this is where I prefer
to leave it, this plain, small poem, digging and breathing like
it wants to avoid some classic fate or some failure of will or some
defect of character, bragging into all the noise and commotion, all
the rips and undertows, that there will be a last time, but this is not it.

Tonight It's a Word

My joints are throbbing from holding my body together. It's
the only way, some nights, I know I'm alive. I am profoundly
happy. Keats is here in his letters, and Saint John of the Cross,
and a paper about stars that are so dense that normal atoms
cannot survive in them. It's one of those summer nights,
an onshore flow bringing the savor of plankton into
the skylight of my little room—nothing I would call a breeze,
just a whiff of the sea from far off, and the private song
of the ceiling fan, and a shy hum from somewhere deep
in the sleeping house, and notebooks and the cat. Just think,
my heart was starving once. Maybe that was this afternoon.
Now maybe a little skiff floats somewhere on the glassy harbor,
maybe its anchor is kedged deep in the bottom sand. Maybe
gulls sleep huddled in its shadows. Maybe somewhere,
in some narrow street, two people kiss and surprise themselves,
or maybe Keats is falling in love again, or maybe St. John
of the Cross is just sitting down to his bread and his wine when
a hidden bird begins singing in the dark hedge. I didn't make
the world. I would never have known enough about the stars and
the atoms. I would never have gone beyond my famished heart.
If I listen very hard, I can hear the silence under absolutely everything.
Or maybe it's a prayer. Or maybe tonight it's only a word. Maybe it's *yes*.

Many Trumpets and Maracas

There are no tanks rolling here, there is no army, no one
is throwing stones. I understand that this is a particular
moment and a particular place. All along the trail to the river,
lizards freeze with a sideways eye, eyes a profound black
against the head and body of emerald and neon. And the path
through heliconia and philodendron and thorny palm opens out,
and someone has built a bodega by the river since I was here last:
warm beers and radio music at the jungle edge—many
trumpets and maracas. Then the little river running out
to the surf, the surf high and translucent when the waves jack
on the river bar, like bottle glass, then like cream. There is one
other rider in the break when I get there. He puts some of his
language against some of my language, I put some of my language
against some of his language. We help each other out. *Big rocks
here on the bar, he says. Go right when you have a choice.*
He wants to know the general term for his Churchills. I tell him *fins*.
The waves are pumping. He goes, I go, he goes, I go. It is like that
for a while. I pay attention. My thoughts, though they shouldn't be,
are still long, long thoughts, but there is little enough thinking here,
and you cannot hear the trumpets or the maracas, for the wind is blowing
white curtains off the tops of the waves and the waves are rumbling.
I paddle out over a crest and a needle-fish jumps, inches from my face,
a flash, all silver and pill-eyed. You might say oceanography or physics,
or hydraulics, or meteorology, but you'd be better off saying *right* or *left*
or *outside*. Or if you stretch it a bit, you might simply say blue like the sky,
or white like the clouds or just green. Green like that green coming for you.

The Sighing of the Ruddy Ground-Dove

Then I am exhausting green, exhausting the books full of green
because the world under me demands that kind of labor as
I am bouncing down through rough cumulous in the scary
little plane, so cramped, like in the back seat of an old car,
and down over the shining river, jade and malachite, and
every variegation, every disquietude of green and shadow
with the sun falling like crochet on the tops of the jungle,
and then bumping onto the narrow cut strip among the old
growth which, I have been told, is all going off forever to
someplace unspeakable, one and one-half trees per second.
And of course I always wanted the world to be in every poem,
even if it had to go crazy and pace and break down the edges,
for *I* am in the world, and I am always pacing and trying to
break down *its* edges, but that is not the way things work—
and so I climb into the back of the covered truck, and we grind
slow and hot up the ruts of the dirt road, past a man on a horse
and past a man on a donkey, and past a woman carrying water,
and deep into steaming forest and its million sounds and its
million kinds of light and strangeness. I'm not certain that the mind
saves anything, not even the thunder of the howler monkey or
the sighing of the ruddy ground-dove, except maybe for a moment,
and then only in a particular way. Here, the trees would eat the sky
if they could, the vines and lianas would pull down your cities.
You might think of it as one edge of something. Or you might
think of it as the font of pure oxygen, which would explain why
my voice is lighting up with one strange note after another,
a narcosis green, a confusion green, a calamity green, a dripping
heat green, a slime mud green, impossible to keep any single
craving green from tumbling into the arms of any other starving
green, and then I can see that no matter what I might assemble
or disperse, there is no clear way to tell just what this world is.

Green

And so I swam out to where the turtles live,
about a half mile off shore where the bottom
is lava and coral and struck with canyons of white sand.
The turtles are green and as big as the wheels
on an automobile or a truck. They like to glide
about twenty feet down, where they are sovereign
and agile and untouchable, but I was raised on the ocean
and I still know how to go down deep and stay there:
You float for a minute and go limp, and you breathe deeply
through the tube you hold clenched in your teeth.
Then you let everything out and slip under.
You move with the languor and sorrow of turtles.
You practice their ease, their cumbersome grace.
What is the mind of turtle? In one moment I saw two
come together and appear to kiss. I guess they were saying,
Come on down, let's see if you've got anything left. I kicked easy.
I blew the pain out of my ears more than once. I chased
one in simple play, in a spiral, tighter and tighter. Maybe
they were amused. Maybe they wanted to kill me.
An old bull came by, aloof, a beard of barnacles on
his hangman's head. How many times down for me? Ten?
Thirty? How long like a stick on the choppy water?
Well, I admired how the turtles watched me over their shoulders,
I appreciated their curiosity and their disdain. When you are
down like that, you get two signals. The first is a quick
need to breathe. You let that one go, blow out a little,
and the urge passes—or you get used to it. Then you
are empty but touched with dementia. Then you can speak
with the god of the sea in his crown of weeds or his goddess and
her many shells. Then you are amphibious and immortal and you
can join the turtle dance again, or just hold to a piece of coral
and hang like a tail of kelp in the eddies. When you

understand that you are in your home and need never leave,
you'd better look up. Then you see how far that old world is
and how much work you have to do. And so
I pulled my way up from the deep, kicking and kicking,
and the turtles just watched, not caring much. I lay
on the surface and breathed and rested until I could lift
my head to see where the current had set me.
The sun was red and swollen and low behind me,
and the long clouds were purpling under their hems and edges.
Now there was so much I had to leave.
And now there was so much I had to get back to.
The beach was a blur of tiny palms, the ocean was windy and warm.
And so I stroked, slow and easy. And so I kicked and I kicked.

ALICE JAMES BOOKS has been publishing exclusively poetry since 1973. One of the few presses in the country that is run collectively, the cooperative selects manuscripts for publication through both regional and national annual competitions. New regional authors become active members of the cooperative, participating in the editorial decisions of the press. The press, which historically has placed an emphasis on publishing women poets, was named for Alice James, sister of William and Henry, whose fine journal and gift for writing went unrecognized within her lifetime.

TYPESET AND DESIGNED BY MIKE BURTON

PRINTED BY THOMSON-SHORE